Selected Duets

for CLARINET

Published in Two Volumes:

- **VOLUME I (Easy-Medium)**
- **VOLUME II (Advanced)**

Compiled and Edited

by H. VOXMAN

RUBANK®

HAL•LEONARD®
CORPORATION
7777 W. BLUEMOUND RD. P.O. BOX 13819 MILWAUKEE, WI 53213

PREFACE

Duet playing affords the student the most intimate form of ensemble experience. The problems of technic, tone quality, intonation, and ensemble balance are brought into the sharpest relief. Careful attention must be given to style as indicated by the printed page and as demanded by the intangibles of good taste.

Mastery of the art of duet playing leads easily and naturally to competent performance in the larger ensembles. The numerous works included in this volume have been selected for the purpose of introducing the clarinetist to the finest in two-part ensemble literature and acquainting him with a diversity of musical forms and expressions.

H. Voxman

●

CONTENTS

●

SEVENTEEN DUETS

Selected from the Works of Klosé

KLOSÉ

8

11

KLOSÉ

TWELVE DUETS

Selected from the Works of Magnani

MAGNANI

Moderato

Allegretto non troppo

MAGNANI

Andantino mosso

MAGNANI

Largo assai (in 3)

MAGNANI

Allegro con spirito

MAGNANI

Andante grazioso

MAGNANI

(1) Play the grace notes on the beat.

Tempo di Gavotta

MAGNANI

12

SEVEN DUETS IN CANON FORM

Selected from Studies in Canon Form by Saro

CANON IN UNISON

SARO

CANON IN A TONE LOWER

SARO

CANON IN A THIRD LOWER

Slowly

SARO

3

CANON IN A FOURTH HIGHER

SARO

CANON IN A FOURTH LOWER

SARO

CANON IN A FIFTH HIGHER

SARO

CANON IN A FIFTH LOWER

SARO

NINE DUETS

Selected from the Works of Berr

BERR

Moderato

BERR

Andante

BERR

BERR

Moderato

BERR

6

2nd time

rall.

Andante

BERR

TWENTY-TWO DUETS

Selected from the Works of
Gliere, Hohmann, Pleyel, Spohr, Volckmar and others

VIOTTI

36

Moderato (in 3)

GLIERE

2

Animato

Allegretto

FRÖHLICH

Menuet

HAYDN

41

Menuetto
con moto

PLEYEL

44

Allegro moderato

CORELLI

RONDO

PLEYEL

Lento

GLIERE

10

HOHMANN

GEMINIANI

Allegretto

HOHMANN

Tempo di menuetto

BRUNI

Allegretto

Cossack Melody

18

SPOHR

Allegro

19

Allegro

PLEYEL

20

Allegro

FUGUE

VOLCKMAR

SEVEN DUETS

Selected from the Works of Mozart

MOZART

MOZART

Menuetto

3

MOZART

MOZART

Polonaise

MOZART